D0849833

HIP-HOP STARS

RUN-DMC

HIP-HOP STARS

Beastie Boys
Sean Combs
Missy Elliott
Eminem
Jay-Z   **LL Cool J**
    Queen Latifah
    Run-DMC
Tupac Shakur
Russell Simmons

RUN-DMC

Louise Chipley Slavicek

CHELSEA HOUSE
PUBLISHERS
An imprint of Infobase Publishing

RUN-DMC

Copyright © 2007 by Infobase Publishing

Chelsea House
An imprint of Infobase Publishing
132 West 31st Street
New York, NY 10001

Library of Congress Cataloging-in-Publication Data

Slavicek, Louise Chipley, 1956-
  Run-DMC / Louise Chipley Slavicek.
     p. cm. — (Hip-hop stars)
  Includes bibliographical references (p.   ), discography (p.   ), and index.
  ISBN-13: 978-0-7910-9499-0 (hardcover)
  ISBN-10: 0-7910-9499-5 (hardcover)
  1. Run-D.M.C. (Musical group)—Juvenile literature.   2. Rap musicians—
United States—Biography—Juvenile literature.   I. Title.   II. Series.

  ML3930.R86S43 2007
  782.421649092'2—dc22   2007001461
  [B]

Chelsea House books are available at special discounts when purchased in bulk quantities
for businesses, associations, institutions, or sales promotions. Please call our Special Sales
Department in New York at (212) 967-8800 or (800) 322-8755.

You can find Chelsea House on the World Wide Web at http://www.chelseahouse.com
Text design by Erik Lindstrom
Cover design by Ben Peterson

Printed in the United States of America

Bang NMSG 10 9 8 7 6 5 4 3 2 1

This book is printed on acid-free paper.

All links and Web addresses were checked and verified to be correct at the time of
publication. Because of the dynamic nature of the Web, some addresses and links
may have changed since publication and may no longer be valid.

CONTENTS

Hip-Hop: A Brief History

Like the air we breathe, hip-hop seems to be everywhere. The lifestyle that many thought would be a passing fad has, three decades later, grown to become a permanent part of world culture. Hip-hop artists have become some of today's heroes, replacing the comic book worship of decades past and joining athletes and movie stars as the people kids dream of being. Names like 50 Cent, P. Diddy, Russell Simmons, Jay-Z, Foxy Brown, Snoop Dogg, and Flavor Flav now ring as familiar as Elvis, Babe Ruth, Marilyn Monroe, and Charlie Chaplin.

While the general public knows many of the names, videos, and songs branded by the big companies that make them popular, it's also important to know the holy trinity, the founding fathers of hip-hop: Kool DJ Herc, Grandmaster

Flash, and Afrika Bambaataa. All are deejays who played and presented the records that rappers and dancers delighted themselves upon. Bambaataa single-handedly stopped the gang wars in the 1970s with the themes of peace, unity, love and having fun.

Hip-hop is simply a term for a form of artistic creativity that was spawned in New York City—more precisely the Bronx—in the early to mid-1970s. Amidst the urban decay in the areas where black and Hispanic people dwelled, economic, educational, and environmental resources were depleted. Jobs and businesses were all but moved away. Living conditions were of a lower standard than the rest of the city and country. Last but not least, art and sports programs in the schools were the first to be cut for the sake of lowering budgets; thus music classes, teaching the subject's history and techniques were all but lost.

From these ashes, like a phoenix, rose an art form. Through the love of technology and records found in family collections or even those tossed out on the street, the deejay emerged. Different from the ones heard on the radio, these folk were innovating a style that was popular on the island of Jamaica. Two turntables kept the music continuous, with the occasional voice on top of the records. This was the very humble beginning of rap music.

Rap music is actually two distinct words: rap and music. "Rap" is the vocal application that is used on top of the music. On a vocal spectrum, it is between talking and singing and is one of the few alternatives for vocalizing to emerge in the last 50 years. It's important to know that inventors and artists are side by side in the importance of music's development. Let's remember that inventor Thomas A. Edison created the first recording with "Mary Had a Little Lamb" in 1878, possibly in New Jersey, the same state as the first rap recording—Sugarhill Gang's "Rapper's Delight"—was made more than 100 years later, in 1979.

It's hard to separate the importance of history, science, language arts, and education when discussing music. Because of the social silencing of black people in the United States from slavery in the 1600s to civil rights in the 1960s, much sentiment, dialogue, and soul is wrapped within their cultural expression of music. In eighteenth-century New Orleans, slaves gathered on Sundays in Congo Square to socialize and play music. Within this captivity many dialects, customs, and styles combined with instrumentation, vocals, and rhythm to form a musical signal or code of preservation. These are the foundations of jazz and the blues. Likewise, it's impossible to separate hip-hop and rap music from the creativity of the past. Look within the expression and words of black music, and you'll get a reflection of history itself. The four creative elements of hip-hop—emceeing (the art of vocalization); deejaying (the musician-like manipulation of records); break dancing (the body expression of the music); and graffiti (the drawn graphic expression of the culture)—have been intertwined in the community before and since slavery.

However, just because these expressions were introduced by the black–Hispanic underclass, doesn't mean that others cannot create or appreciate hip-hop. Hip-hop is a cultural language used best to unite the human family all around the world. To peep the global explosion, one need not search far. Starting just north of the U.S. border, Canadian hip-hop has featured indigenous rappers who are infusing different language and dialect flows into their work, from Alaskan Eskimo to French flowing cats from Montreal and the rest of the Quebec's provincial region. Few know that France for many years has been the second largest hip-hop nation, measured not just by high sales numbers, but also by a very political philosophy. Hip-hop has been alive and present since the mid-1980s in Japan and other Asian countries. Australia has been a hotbed in welcoming world rap acts, and it has also created its own vibrant hip-hop scene, with the reminder of its government's takeover of indigenous people reflected in every rapper's flow and rhyme. As a rhythm of the people, the continents of Africa and South America (especially Ghana, Senegal, and South Africa, Brazil, Surinam, and Argentina) have long mixed traditional homage into the new beats and rhyme of this millennium.

Hip-hop has been used to help Brazilian kids learn English when school systems failed to bridge the difficult language gap of Portuguese and patois to American English. It has entertained and enlightened youth and has engaged political discussion in society, continuing the tradition of the African griots (storytellers) and folk singers.

For the past 25 years, hip-hop has been bought, sold, followed, loved, hated, praised, and blamed. History has shown that other cultural music forms in the United States have been just as misunderstood and held up to public scrutiny. The history of the people who originated the art form can be found in the music itself. The timeline of recorded rap music spans more than a quarter century, and that alone is history in itself.

Presidents, kings, queens, fame, famine, infamy, from the great wall of China to the Berlin wall, food, drugs, cars, hate, and love have been rhymed and scratched. This gives plenty reason for social study. And I don't know what can be more fun than learning the history of something so relevant to young minds and souls, as music.

October 30, 2002

On a cold, rainy evening just before Halloween in 2002, an assassin's bullet put an end to what was arguably the most influential hip-hop group of all time: Run-DMC. At approximately 7:30 P.M. on October 30, Run-DMC's long-time DJ, Jason Mizell—a.k.a. Jam Master Jay—was shot in the head at point-blank range in his New York City recording studio by an intruder. Jay was seated on a couch in the lounge playing video games when a masked man burst into his Merrick Boulevard studio and opened fire with a .40-caliber pistol.

Thirty-seven-year-old Mizell died instantly, only blocks from where he and his band mates and close friends, rappers Joseph "Run" Simmons and Darryl "DMC" McDaniels, had

Run-DMC, pictured here in 1987, were hip-hop pioneers who brought the art form to the mainstream by blending rap with rock and heavy metal. The group broke ground for today's hip-hop acts.

grown up in the middle class, mostly African-American suburb of Hollis, Queens. To this day, both the identity and the motive of Mizell's murderer remain unknown.

When Jam Master Jay died in late 2002, he, Run, and DMC were just a few months away from celebrating their twentieth anniversary as a group. To the dismay of Run-DMC's many fans in the United States and around the world, within days of Jay's funeral Simmons announced that the group was officially retired. "I can't get out on stage with a new deejay," Run explained to the press. "I don't know any other way but with the original three members."

A STRING OF "FIRSTS"

According to some music critics and chroniclers of popular culture, Run-DMC played a greater role in shaping the sound and style of rap than any other hip-hop group before or since. When the trio first appeared on New York City's emerging hip-hop scene in the early 1980s, their stripped-down musical arrangements, edgy lyrics, and casual, straight-off-the street look immediately captured the imagination of the black community and spawned a host of imitators. By the mid-eighties, Run-DMC's innovative melding of rap with heavy metal had launched them into the musical mainstream, making them the first hip-hop group to gain widespread popularity among a non–African-American audience.

During the 1980s, Run-DMC attained a number of important "firsts" in addition to being the first rap group with broad crossover appeal, achievements that helped make hip-hop one of the most powerful cultural movements of the late twentieth and early twenty-first centuries in America. With a recording career spanning nearly two decades and more than 25 million albums sold, Run-DMC was the first rap group to have a gold album (the self-named *Run-DMC* in 1984), a platinum album (*King of Rock* in 1985), and a multiplatinum album (*Raising Hell* in 1986). They were also the first rappers to have a music video played on MTV, to be nominated for a Grammy award, and to appear on the cover of America's

Jason "Jam Master Jay" Mizell was tragically murdered in his Queens recording studio on October 30, 2002. Jay's friends and partners for nearly thirty years, Run and DMC, decided to disband the group rather than attempt to replace him.

premier rock magazine, *Rolling Stone.* By 1986, with the release of their third album, *Raising Hell,* and its smash hit single, "Walk This Way," recorded with rock stars Steven Tyler and Joe Perry of Aerosmith, Run-DMC was the most famous and successful hip-hop group in the world.

In the years following the phenomenal popularity of *Raising Hell,* however, the group confronted a series of daunting challenges: fierce competition from the new "gangsta" rappers such as N.W.A., declining record sales and concert bookings, lackluster reviews, drug and alcohol addictions, and a criminal trial. Ironically, in 2002, the year that Jason Mizell died, things were finally beginning to look up for the trio. All three members had gotten their personal lives back on track, and that summer, Run-DMC opened for Aerosmith, their "Walk This Way" collaborators, on a major national tour. Encouraged by the enthusiastic reception they received everywhere they performed on the sellout tour, Run, DMC, and Jay began planning a twentieth-anniversary album. Then, the unimaginable happened: Jam Master Jay was shot and killed.

For nearly three years following the senseless murder of Jam Master Jay, Run and DMC kept out of the public view except to participate in memorials to their slain bandmate. But neither rapper was ready to abandon the music that had been an integral part of their lives since they were thirteen years old. In 2005 and 2006, respectively, Run, or "Rev Run" as he now called himself, and DMC each released a solo rap album. It remains to be seen whether Rev Run and DMC can build successful solo musical careers, but the legacy of the celebrated rap group that the two friends helped found in 1983 still endures.

When Jason Mizell, Joseph Simmons, and Darryl McDaniels released their first hit single, "It's Like That," the record's minimalist arrangement and hard-hitting lyrics not only introduced a whole new element into rap but also helped move hip-hop music and culture out of its New York City birthplace and into the national consciousness. As Jay's longtime friend from Hollis, rapper and DJ Wendell "Hurricane" Fite, told author Ronin Ro shortly after Jay's death, Run-DMC "opened the doors for rap music.... Without Run-DMC, I really don't know how far hip-hop would have gone."

Hip-Hop Comes to Hollis

During the early 1970s, while the African-American cultural movement known as hip-hop was emerging in New York City's poorest borough, the Bronx, two brothers by the names of Joseph (Joey) and Russell Simmons were growing up just a 15-minute drive away in the comfortably middle-class neighborhood of Hollis, Queens.

By the end of the decade, hip-hop—and particularly rap, the movement's chief musical expression—had made its way from the crime-ridden ghettos of the Bronx to the tree-lined streets of Hollis, and Joey and Russell's lives would never be the same again. Although they were too young to be part of the local scene at its inception, they would still be affected by the movement.

HIP-HOP'S BEGINNINGS: GRAFFITI AND BREAK DANCING

Scholars cannot pinpoint the precise date of hip-hop's birth. By 1975, however, the four fundamental elements of the new movement—graffiti, break dancing, deejaying, and rapping—had all made their first appearance in the impoverished and mostly black neighborhoods of the South Bronx, generally considered as the cradle of hip-hop culture.

The first two components of hip-hop culture to emerge were graffiti and break dancing. Graffiti has its roots in the late 1960s, when self-styled "writers" began using permanent markers or paint to make distinctive designs—often their initials or combinations of letters and numbers—on the sides of subway cars, buildings, bridges, and other public and private surfaces in New York City. Graffiti was an especially common sight in the gang-infested slums of the South Bronx, where members of rival gangs used cans of spray paint to "tag" their territories with their gang's name or colors. Despite its association with street violence, when several leading Manhattan art dealers began displaying graffiti-inspired works in their galleries during the mid-seventies, graffiti seemed to be on its way to becoming a respected art form.

New York's graffiti craze would prove short lived, however. Convinced that graffiti was vandalism not art, city authorities launched a determined and largely successful campaign against the practice during the early 1980s, complete with undercover police squads, guard dogs, and paint-dissolving acid baths.

Break dancing, a high-energy, acrobatic style of dancing, developed among young black New Yorkers around the same time that graffiti was first taking hold in the city. This second element of hip-hop culture featured eye-catching movements such as locking and popping in which the B-boys and B-girls (male and female break-dancers) "locked" a leg or other body part into position before abruptly "popping" it out again. Soon break-dance "crews" made up of young ghetto residents began competing in local contests and talent shows. Like graffiti, break dancing was especially popular in the gang-ridden neighborhoods of the South Bronx, where rival B-boy gangs staged dance competitions to gain status and respect or for control of disputed territory. By the early eighties, break dancing, like graffiti, was already on the decline, having been replaced by new dances such as the Freak and the Robot.

THE RISE OF DEEJAYING AND RAP

The most influential and long-lasting of hip-hop's street-based art forms proved to be musical: deejaying—or turntabling—and rap. Deejaying (short for disc jockeying) was the first musical element of hip-hop to develop. Until the hip-hop era, a DJ or "spinner" was someone who announced and played records for a radio station or dance party. In contrast, hip-hop DJs were musicians themselves with the phonograph being their chief instrument.

By the early seventies, spinners in the South Bronx were experimenting with the mechanics of record playing in order to create an entirely new sound. Above all, these new-style DJ-musicians focused on manipulating what came to be known as the break beat, the part of a dance song in which the singing stopped but the percussion continued. In order to extend this most exciting and danceable part of a song for as long as possible, hip-hop spinners used two turntables and placed a copy of the same record on each one. By rapidly cutting back and forth between the two records, a DJ could sustain the break-beat segment indefinitely.

Soon pioneering DJs such as South Bronx natives D. J. Hollywood and Afrika Bambaataa began to add rhythmic accents to the music they played by "scratching" the record—a technique in which the disc is quickly slid back and forth underneath the turntable's stylus, or needle.

While the new hip-hop DJs were experimenting with turntable and record manipulation, the element of hip-hop

Hip-hop began as a blend of four art forms: rapping, deejaying, graffiti, and break dancing. Armed with a boombox and a piece of cardboard for padding, many breakdancers set up makeshift stages in parks, squares, subways, and anywhere they could draw a crowd to show off their moves and earn a few dollars.

that has often been described as the heart and soul of the entire movement—rap—was also emerging in the ghettos of the South Bronx. A musical style featuring rhythmic and often rhyming speech, rap has deep roots in African and African-American culture. Many scholars have linked modern rappers to the traditional Western African griot—a traveling troubadour who educated and entertained audiences with stories that he usually chanted in a rhythmic fashion.

Rap has also been tied to African-American word games dating back to the slave era, including "the dozens," in which one player taunts another by insulting or poking fun at his or her family, and "signifying," in which players brag about their own assets or accomplishments while belittling those of their opponents.

The influence of both African and African-American culture on modern rap is clearly strong. Yet most scholars agree that the musical genre's most immediate source is Caribbean: the Jamaican custom of "toasting." By the 1960s, toasting—or talking over dance songs—had become a regular feature at Jamaican street parties, particularly in the island's capital city of Kingston. Instead of just selecting and introducing songs, Jamaican DJs grabbed a microphone while the music was still playing and "shouted out" greetings to friends or acquaintances in the audience, recited improvised chants or rhymes, or boasted about themselves or their family members.

Toasting was first brought to the United States during the early seventies by a young Jamaican immigrant to the South Bronx named Clive Campbell. Performing under the stage name Kool DJ Herc, Campbell became famous throughout the borough for his popular block parties and park jams. One of the first DJs to experiment with isolating and extending a track's break beat, Kool Herc would talk over the long breaks he created in a rhythmic singsong. Like the DJs in his Jamaican homeland, Herc entertained his listeners by calling out to buddies in the crowd, reciting limericks, or bragging outrageously about his prowess as a musician or lover.

Intrigued by his energetic stage presence and innovative style, young people turned out in droves to see the teenaged spinner. Soon other African-American DJs in the Bronx began to imitate Kool Herc's unconventional methods, and toasting—or rapping, as it was beginning to be known—spread rapidly through New York City's black ghettos.

RUSSELL SIMMONS DISCOVERS HIP-HOP MUSIC

Although hip-hop culture was born in the South Bronx, two of the most influential figures in the history of rap—music producer Russell Simmons (born October 4, 1957) and his brother, Run-DMC cofounder Joseph Simmons (born November 14, 1964)—hailed from a solidly middle-class section of New York City: the suburb of Hollis, Queens. In many ways, Hollis, with its neat aluminum-sided houses and meticulously manicured lawns, was a world apart from the dilapidated tenements and garbage-strewn streets of the South Bronx.

Yet for all their differences, Hollis and the South Bronx had two important features in common when the Simmons brothers were growing up. Both areas were overwhelmingly black and both had a large and active population of young people who were keenly attuned to the latest trends in African-American culture, particularly in the realm of popular music. Consequently, when hip-hop swept through the slums of the Bronx during the first half of the 1970s, it was only a matter of time before it found its way southward to Hollis.

The one individual most responsible for bringing the heart of the South Bronx's new hip-hop culture to Hollis—deejaying and rap—was Russell "Rush" Simmons. Russell may have been raised in the suburbs, but he was definitely streetwise. Hollis was only a 50-cent subway ride from the drug-infested ghettos of the Bronx and Harlem, and during the seventies when Russell was a teenager, illegal drugs, particularly marijuana, were readily available in his hometown. To earn some pocket money, Russell, like many of his high school classmates, sold "nickel bags" of marijuana. For a short time, he was even a warlord in the Seven Immortals, a notorious street gang with chapters all over New York City.

After graduation, Russell enrolled in the Harlem branch of the City College of New York at the urging of his college-educated parents, Daniel and Evelyn Simmons. At City College, Simmons majored in sociology, but his chief interest was

Hip-hop was born on the streets of the South Bronx in the 1970s. From poverty, a blending of cultures, close quarters, and creative inspiration came a new, totally original art that has not only continued, but grown stronger three decades later.

Harlem's lively nightclub scene. One evening during the fall of his junior year in 1977, Simmons heard his very first rapper, DJ Eddie Cheeba, at a trendy Harlem dance club. Simmons, who had been financing his club-hopping habit by selling fake cocaine, was not only genuinely smitten by the new music but also sensed an outstanding money-making opportunity. He decided on the spot to organize and promote rap concerts and dance parties in his home borough of Queens, where hip-hop was still largely unknown as of late 1977.

QUEENS'S NUMBER-ONE RAPPER

Simmons soon recruited several of his college buddies to assist him with his new business venture, including freshman Kurt Walker, a part-time DJ and aspiring rapper. After persuading Walker to adopt the stage name Kurtis Blow, Simmons began renting out halls in Hollis and elsewhere in Queens. With the help of his college friends and younger brother Joey, Simmons passed out thousands of flyers for his parties in which he shamelessly touted 18-year-old Kurtis Blow—a Harlem native—as Queens's number-one rapper.

With Russell promoting up to three parties in a single weekend, Kurtis Blow was a frequent visitor at the Simmons' household, often sleeping over after a late show. Much impressed by the suave young showman, 13-year-old Joey Simmons was eager

THE CHANGING FACE OF HOLLIS

Although Joseph and Russell Simmons' hometown of Hollis remained integrated into the early seventies, as more and more middle-class African Americans fled the crime-ridden inner-city neighborhoods for the Queens suburb, to the dismay of their father, Daniel Sr., Hollis's white residents began to move out, as Bill Adler recounts in *Tougher Than Leather: The Rise of Run DMC*:

> **Hollis was 70 percent white when Daniel Simmons moved there with his pregnant wife Evelyn and two oldest sons—Daniel Jr., 11, and Russell, 7—in November 1964, just 14 days before Joseph—who would one day be known as Run—was born. Daniel Sr.'s written remembrance paints Hollis as "a place made for people who dream of a green lawn, a patio, and genial people**

to learn everything he could from Kurtis about the exciting new world of deejaying and rapping. Soon the eighth grader had set up a studio in his house's spacious attic complete with two old turntables and a large stack of disco, R&B (rhythm and blues), and soul records. With single-minded determination, he taught himself how to seamlessly extend a track's break beat by cutting back and forth between the two turntables with lightening speed. Joey also worked diligently on his rapping skills, making up and reciting dozens of humorous and boastful rhymes patterned on those Kurtis used in his shows.

By the beginning of 1978, Joey's dedication and burgeoning abilities as a DJ and rapper had made a big impression on Russell. Consequently, when Russell heard that DJ Hollywood, one of Kurtis Blow's chief competitors on the

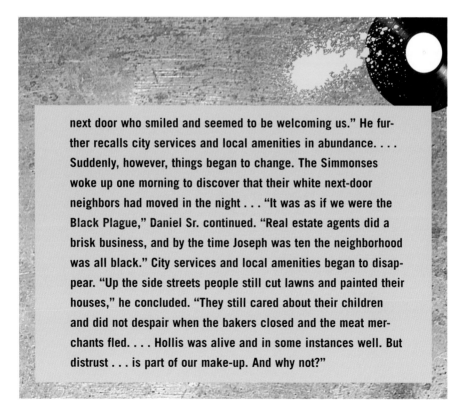

next door who smiled and seemed to be welcoming us." He further recalls city services and local amenities in abundance. . . . Suddenly, however, things began to change. The Simmonses woke up one morning to discover that their white next-door neighbors had moved in the night . . . "It was as if we were the Black Plague," Daniel Sr. continued. "Real estate agents did a brisk business, and by the time Joseph was ten the neighborhood was all black." City services and local amenities began to disappear. "Up the side streets people still cut lawns and painted their houses," he concluded. "They still cared about their children and did not despair when the bakers closed and the meat merchants fled. . . . Hollis was alive and in some instances well. But distrust . . . is part of our make-up. And why not?"

rap party circuit, now had a young assistant spinner working with him, he decided to hire Joey as Walker's helper. Although neither he nor his older brother could not have imagined it at the time, at the tender age of 13, Joey Simmons was about to embark on what would prove to be a remarkably successful and enduring career as a hip-hop performer.

DJ Run and Easy D

By the time that Joey began performing with Kurtis Blow, Russell Simmons's party promotion business was booming, and he was booking shows in all five of New York City's boroughs. Joey's very first performance in the winter of 1978 was in the heart of Manhattan at the Diplomat, a rather run-down hotel just off Times Square.

In his flyers for the dance party, Russell billed Joey as Kurtis Blow's son, DJ Run. Joey's colorful stage name was meant to call attention to the young DJs lightning-fast "cutting" abilities, Russell explained to his little brother. He also chose the name "DJ Run," Russell teased, because Joey was forever running off at the mouth. Joey was thrilled with his catchy new nickname, and soon just about everybody

Born August 9, 1959, Curtis Walker was shepherded by promoter Russell Simmons and renamed Kurtis Blow before becoming the first rapper to sign with a major label. Kurtis Blow was also known for mentoring young rap acts in hip-hop's early days, and he influenced the genre by working behind the scenes after his own recording career waned. He is considered the first commercially successful rap artist.

in Hollis had begun referring to the talkative 13-year-old as Run.

Although Joey was originally hired to help Kurtis Blow with the turntables, Russell was so taken with the teen's rapping skills that Run ended up spending most of his time on stage trading rhymes with his "dad." At the start of each show, Run would introduce himself to the crowd with what quickly became his signature rhyme: "I'm DJ Run, son of a gun/Always plays music and has big fun/Not that old, but that's all right/Make all other emcees bite all night." (In hip-hop slang, to "bite" means to steal an especially clever or humorous rhyme from another rapper or "emcee." Rappers were often referred to as "emcees," or MCs— short for master of ceremonies—during the seventies.)

Self-assured and outgoing, Run was not in the least bit intim- idated by performing in public. In fact, he clearly relished being the center of attention. Nonetheless, Run soon discovered that his new job could be exhausting—he and Russell often did not arrive home from a weekend gig until breakfast time—and also danger- ous. At two dance clubs in Queens, Le Chalet and Fantasia, where he and Kurtis Blow regularly performed, "people used to shoot guns all the time," Run later told writer Bill Adler. "You'd hear a cap go off—*Pah!*—and everybody'd go running a different way. If I was onstage, I'd just put the mike down and step to the side. One day after a show, they were shooting outside of Fantasia, and Kurt and I both dove under a car."

ENTER DARRYL MCDANIELS

Shortly after he started working with Kurtis Blow, Run made friends with another Hollis teen who was destined to play a cru- cial role in both his personal and professional lives: Darryl "D" McDaniels. Although they attended the same elementary school, the boys did not really get to know one another until the spring of 1978 when they played basketball together on a local Police Athletic League team. The two eighth graders quickly discov- ered that they had something in common besides their love for basketball: a deep fascination with hip-hop music.

D became intrigued with the gritty new street music after listening to a taped performance by the famous South Bronx DJ and rapper Grandmaster Flash. Drawing—and especially cartooning—had long been D's favorite pastime. Now the quiet and studious teen had a new passion. Using two beat-up turntables and an audio mixer donated by his older brother Alford, D taught himself how to cut, scratch, and backspin (move a record on the turntable so that certain phrases or beats are repeated) just like Grandmaster Flash. D spent many happy hours experimenting with his phonographs and mixer in his "laboratory," as he liked to call his makeshift basement studio.

When he found out that his new friend Run was Kurtis Blow's assistant, D pled with his mother, Bannah, to let him attend the pair's shows at Le Chalet on Hillside Avenue and at other local nightclubs. But Bannah McDaniels refused, insisting that her son was too young to mingle with such a rough crowd. So that D would have a chance to hear his performances, Run always asked someone in the audience to record his gigs. Then on Sunday afternoons, he played the tapes for D in the "laboratory," and the boys discussed what had gone well—and what had not—at that weekend's shows.

Soon D and Run were hanging out nearly every day. Usually they would play some basketball and then head for the McDaniels's basement to practice their rapping and spinning techniques. The two developed elaborate emcee routines in which one would start a rhyme and the other would finish it, and D jokingly dubbed himself DJ Run's sidekick, "Grandmaster Get High." In fact, getting high was something that both boys did frequently. As DMC later admitted in his autobiography, *King of Rock: Respect, Responsibility, and My Life with Run-DMC,* he began smoking marijuana in junior high because he thought that was what he had to do "in order to be down with the older guys, the tough guys, the hard rocks, the B-boys in the neighborhood."

Grandmaster Flash *(above)* innovated DJ techniques and changed music forever. By extending beats and playing bits from various songs to make new songs and sounds, Flash converted turntables into an instrument. His talent led to the founding of pioneering rap group the Furious Five, which influenced nearly every early rap act that followed.

"EASY D"

In September 1978, Run and D headed off to high school. Run enrolled at Andrew Jackson, Hollis's public high school, while D attended Brother Rice, a private Catholic institution in Harlem that his mother hoped would provide a safer and more wholesome environment for her youngest child than Andrew Jackson. Despite attending different schools, the boys continued to spend an enormous amount of time together, especially after Run's parents presented him with two expensive new turntables for his 14th birthday that November.

Though D was enthralled by Run's pricey new audio equipment, during his freshman year at Rice he became increasingly focused on rapping and less and less interested in spinning. An A-student in English with a knack for creative writing, D, or "Easy D" as he now styled himself, always seemed to be working on a new rhyme. He penned rhymes in Run's attic, on the two

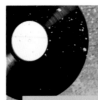

RAPPING IN THE PARK

On most summer weekend evenings in the late seventies and early eighties, hundreds of Hollis teenagers headed to Two-Fifth Park, also known as 192 Park because it was located directly behind Junior High School 192. They were drawn there by the promise of a free concert featuring the exciting new sound of hip-hop DJs and rappers, usually local amateurs eager for a chance to practice their skills before a live audience. In his autobiography, *King of Rock: Respect, Responsibility, and My Life with Run-DMC*, DMC fondly remembers the impromptu park jams of his high school years:

> The DJ usually arrived in a van. It got to the point that when people saw the van, they would get really excited. They knew it was going to be a special evening. The equipment was unloaded, they'd tap into a light pole and steal the electricity from the city, and then it was time for the party to begin. Word would get around quickly that the van had come, and then the park would get packed. By nine-thirty, ten at night, the place would be jammed. You could hear the music for blocks, so anyone who wasn't told by a family member that the van was in the park would usually pick up on it really quick. . . .

buses and three trains he had to take to get from his house to Brother Rice, and during the final five minutes of English class, when pupils were encouraged to compose their own poems or stories. Over the course of the school year, D filled seven composition notebooks with rhymes about everything from his favorite brand of sneakers to his mother's cooking.

Impressed by D's originality and sense of humor, Run urged his friend to take the stage with him at impromptu park jams and neighborhood street parties in Hollis. But the tall, bespectacled teen stubbornly refused; he detested performing in public. Ever the optimist, Run was not discouraged. D was bound to outgrow his shyness sooner or later, he figured. When they were older, Run told his buddy, they were going to form their own rap group and become hip-hop stars.

"CHRISTMAS RAPPIN'" AND A BROKEN ARM

By mid-1979, Kurtis Blow had become one of the best-known and popular DJ-emcees in New York City. Russell Simmons, who now formally managed Kurtis Blow, was convinced that the time was right for Kurtis to make a record. Simmons soon persuaded two acquaintances and aspiring music producers to pay for studio time and backup musicians for his pet project, and in August, Kurtis began recording "Christmas Rappin'," a humorous lyric about Santa Claus visiting the ghetto.

While Kurtis was still working on "Christmas Rappin'" in the recording studio, New York City radio stations began playing "Rapper's Delight," a 15-minute single by the Sugarhill Gang, a hip-hop trio from New Jersey. Released by the small African-American-owned label Sugar Hill, "Rapper's Delight" was not the very first rap record—that distinction belongs to the Fatback Band's "King Tim III (Personality Jock)," which came out several months earlier but was largely ignored by radio stations and record buyers alike. "Rapper's Delight," in contrast, was an immediate hit. A lively party jam with an infectious beat, the single quickly climbed to number 36 on

There were several pioneering DJs and rap acts in hip-hop's early days, but without Russell Simmons (*above left*, with his brother Joey "Run" Simmons in 2005) working so hard to get them an audience, it might have been years before the genre took off. A 1999 *Slate* article called hip-hop "the single most significant development in pop culture in the past two decades."

the U.S. pop charts and number 4 on the R&B charts. Greatly heartened by the success of "Rapper's Delight," Simmons and his financial backers launched a vigorous campaign to find a record label for Kurtis Blow's new rap track.

During the autumn of 1979, Simmons pedaled "Christmas Rappin" to 23 record labels and was turned away by every one of them. Convinced that "Rapper's Delight" was a fluke and that rap was nothing more than a passing fad, the big record companies were reluctant to take a chance on the new street music. But Russell Simmons was not the type to give up easily. After identifying PolyGram, home to several leading black R&B artists, as a good fit for Kurtis Blow, he began placing phony orders for "Christmas Rappin" in the record company's system. Persuaded that there was a ready-made market for the single, PolyGram's top brass agreed to release "Christmas Rappin" on their Mercury imprint, making Kurtis Blow the first rapper ever to be signed by a major record label. The wisdom of the executives' decision quickly became evident. Out just in time for the holiday season, "Christmas Rappin" soon sold nearly a half million copies.

Although he had not been involved in making the record, Run was thrilled by the single's success and eager to help Kurtis Blow perform his new hit on stage. He did not have to wait for long. On the strength of the song's impressive sales record, Russell booked Kurtis and Run to perform at concerts in Cleveland, Detroit, and several other out-of-state locales in early 1980. By spring, Kurtis had cut a second single for Mercury, "The Breaks," and had been offered an album deal—a first for a rap artist. Russell, although only a few credits away from earning his bachelor of arts degree, dropped out of college to devote all of his time to managing his flourishing party promotion business and Kurtis's skyrocketing career.

To Run's delight, Russell soon secured a spot for Kurtis Blow and Run on a major national tour as the opening act for the Commodores, a popular R&B group. Then, just a few weeks before the summer tour was scheduled to begin, the unthinkable happened. Run fell down hard while playing basketball and broke his arm. Although Run resolutely taught himself to deejay one-handed, Russell decided that he had no choice but to hire another spinner for the tour. Run's year-and-a-half-long gig as the son of Kurtis Blow had come to an abrupt and disappointing end. But the 15-year-old held fast to his dreams. He and D continued to put in long hours in the Simmons' attic honing their cutting and rapping skills because someday, Run assured his friend, they were going to found a rap group and have hit records and a national tour of their own.

"It's Like That"

About the same time that Run and D were discovering hip-hop, another Hollis teenager and music lover by the name of Jason (Jay) Mizell also found himself drawn to the new sound emanating from the Bronx. A year behind Run and D in school, Jay (born January 21, 1965) moved from Brooklyn to Hollis in 1975. He and his parents, Jesse, a social worker, and Connie, a teacher, lived in a relatively rough part of town near Two-Fifth Park and Hollis Avenue. Brawny and self-confident, Jay was a natural leader, and by age 14 he had formed his own posse, the Hollis Crew, which all but ruled the hallways of Andrew Jackson High. "If you messed with Jason you had a big problem," a former classmate recalled years later. "He was the top dog in school. Nobody touched him."

JAY GETS SERIOUS ABOUT HIS MUSIC

Shortly after moving to Hollis, Jay developed a strong interest in music. He took up both the bass guitar and the drums, and he daydreamed of joining a band. Three years later, he started attending the popular weekend jams at nearby Two-Fifth Park and became fascinated with hip-hop and especially deejaying. Happy to encourage a hobby that kept her rambunctious son at home and out of trouble, Connie Mizell set up two turntables and an audio mixer for Jay in the basement, and he rapidly mastered the skills of cutting, backspinning, and scratching.

It was not until he turned 15, however, that Jay really got serious about his music. One day during his sophomore year in high school, Jay had the bad luck to run into a classmate on Hollis Avenue just moments after the other teen had burglarized a home. Suddenly a police car pulled up next to the two boys. The real burglar bolted, and Jay found himself under arrest on suspicion of breaking and entering. Jay spent the next four days at Spofford Juvenile Facility in the Bronx, a run-down detention center for adolescent boys known for inmate-on-inmate violence and drug dealing right on the premises. Hoping to reassure his worried mother, after his release, Jay made light of his detention, saying that his stint at Spofford had actually been kind of fun. To his dismay, his plan completely backfired. Convinced that her son was well on his way to becoming a hardened criminal, Connie burst into sobs. Years later, Jay would recall his mother's tears that day as marking a major turning point in his life. Determined to make something of himself and regain his parents' respect, Jay began devoting the majority of his free time to music and particularly deejaying.

JAZZY JASE

By the spring of 1980 when Run Simmons broke his arm and lost his job with Kurtis Blow, Jay had already become one of the most popular and admired DJs in Hollis. Using the stage

Before becoming famous, DMC, Run, and Jam Master Jay (*above, left to right,* in 1985) were simply D, Joey, and Jay, boys who knew each other from school and their local park. The three shared a love of music and made promises for the future that they never forgot.

name Jazzy Jase, he was the main attraction at Two-Fifth Park's free hip-hop jams and had even managed to secure several well-paying gigs at local bars and dance clubs. "It's said that the most gifted dj's knew exactly where to drop the needle simply by reading the grooves on the vinyl," noted David Thigpen in *Jam Master Jay: The Heart of Hip-Hop.* "Jason was one of those who could hit a break right on the mark time after time. He became known for his exceptionally nimble fingers, an instant ability to read audience tastes, and encyclopedic knowledge of musicians and records."

Since Jay's chief interest was deejaying not rapping, at the Two-Fifth jams he was invariably generous about sharing his microphone with young would-be emcees in the crowd. Jay was particular about who he would let join him on stage, however. Consequently, when Jay began regularly offering the microphone to Run, whom he knew from school and playing basketball, Run was grateful. After he and D got their first record deal, he told Jay, they planned to ask him to serve as the DJ for their new group.

D FINALLY PERFORMS IN PUBLIC

Although Jay always made a point of inviting D to rap along with Run during his park jams, D stubbornly refused to take the mike. Still plagued by profound shyness, he was terrified of performing before an audience.

One Friday in early 1981, Run decided the time had come for D to confront his fears head on. Run had managed to land a gig at Le Chalet as the opening act for another rapper. Determined to show off the rap routines he and D had been perfecting in his attic, Run called D shortly before the dance party was scheduled to start. Le Chalet's manager was expecting both of them to perform that evening, he announced, and it was too late for D to back out now. Completely taken off guard, D meekly agreed.

As soon as he hung up the phone, he was filled with dread, DMC recalled in *King of Rock*. "I was so scared," he wrote, "I felt like I was in a daze." D, who had started drinking alcohol when he was still in junior high, decided that the only way to calm his nerves was to get drunk. "Unfortunately," he later confessed in his autobiography, "getting really drunk before performing became a habit that I grew to rely on." Before heading off to meet Run, D downed most of a bottle of whisky. By the time he reached Le Chalet, he could barely see. Indeed, D was so inebriated during his and Run's performance that he ended up rapping with his back to the crowd. The next morning, Run reassured his embarrassed friend that his rhymes were good, but next time he needed to actually look at the audience!

COLLEGE AND A RECORD

During the following year, Run and D performed in public many times—usually for free at local park jams, block parties, or other community events. The two friends still dreamed of forming their own group, but their parents insisted that Run and D attend college first. In the fall of 1982, Run began classes at La Guardia Community College and D at St. John's University, both in New York City. Jay, who had dropped out of Andrew Jackson High to help care for his ill father, had recently earned his general equivalency diploma and enrolled at Queens College. None of the young men had a clear idea of what they wanted to study in college. Pressured by their advisors into declaring a major right away, D half-heartedly selected business management, Jay picked computer science and then immediately regretted not choosing philosophy instead, and Run settled on mortuary science because he had an uncle who was a funeral director.

Although his parents wanted him to focus on his college studies and not on his music, Run nagged his brother Russell incessantly about making a record with him and D. Russell, who had recently formed a music production company with bass player Larry Smith, was looking for new recording artists. Yet while Russell was willing to consider taking on Run as a client, he had a strong bias against D. Reserved and bespectacled D, he was convinced, could never make it as a rapper; both his delivery and his look were all wrong.

Then one night in late 1982, Run called D and told him he needed his help right away. Russell had finally agreed to make a record with Run based on an old rhyme of his called "It's Like That." But the rhyme was much too short for a full-length track. Years later, D recalled the conversation in his autobiography: "'Just write, D,' Joey said. 'I know you can write, 'cause that's all you do. Go home and write about how the world is. Write a bunch of rhymes about that.'" When D showed Run what he had written the next day, Run was ecstatic. Russell was going to

"IT'S LIKE THAT" / "SUCKER MCS"

In the first song that they ever recorded as Run-DMC, "It's Like That," Darryl McDaniels and Joseph Simmons rap about the grim reality of life in the ghettos and hold up self-improvement as the only way out. In "Sucker MCs," the "B" or flip side of their first record, the two brag outrageously about their own emceeing skills while putting down, or dissin' (short for disrespecting), their competition.

EXCERPT FROM "IT'S LIKE THAT" (1983)
Unemployment at a record high
People coming, people going, people born to die
Don't ask me, because I don't know why
But it's like that, and that's the way it is.

EXCERPT FROM "SUCKER MCS" (1983)
You're a five dollar boy and I'm a million dollar man
You're a sucker emcee and you're my fan
You try to bite rhymes, all lines are mine
You're a sucker emcee in a pair of Calvin Kleins.

Run-DMC came together as a group after years of perfecting rhymes and beats and practicing their craft at local clubs and block parties.

like the new lyrics so much that he was bound to let D make the record with him, Run assured his friend.

"IT'S LIKE THAT"/"SUCKER MCS"

Run was right. After hearing D's gritty yet literate lyrics for "It's Like That," Russell Simmons invited D to rap with his younger brother on the new record. The duo spent the better part of a January night in 1983 recording "It's Like That" and a second song they wrote called "Sucker MCs," with Russell's partner, bassist Larry Smith, handling the arrangements. At Run and D's insistence, neither piece featured even so much as a hint of melody or harmony, just a few bass guitar riffs and a drum beat, and Run and D talking—actually more like shouting—over the track.

Run and D's songs were unlike any rap pieces ever before recorded. The duo's extremely spare arrangements and edgy street style were completely different from the singles produced by the Sugarhill Gang and the handful of other rap groups who had been able to land record deals during the early eighties. In sharp contrast to Run and D's stripped-down tracks, those records typically featured a full studio band and a lively, disco-party sound.

During the winter of 1983, Russell took Run and D's groundbreaking demo tape to every major record label he could think of in the New York area. To his dismay, the record executives were not impressed by Run and D's innovative sound. The duo's minimalist style was alien and monotonous, the executives said, and totally lacking in commercial appeal. Finally, in desperation, Russell paid a visit to Profile Records, a tiny independent label founded by two white hip-hop fans, Cory Robbins and Steve Plotnicki, only two years earlier.

Intrigued by Run and D's innovative, in-your-face approach, Robbins and Plotnicki agreed to sign the twosome under the name Russell had recently given them—Run-DMC— but for only half the money that Simmons had originally requested. As much as he liked Run and D's tracks, Robbins later admitted, he was not at all confident that they would sell.

Because of a prior obligation, Jay had been unable to be at the studio that January night when Run and D recorded "It's Like That" and "Sucker MCs." Run, however, had not forgotten his promise to Jay. As soon as he and D signed with Profile Records, they visited Jay and asked him to be their new group's DJ. To their delight, he agreed, and soon after the trio began practicing together in preparation for their very first show as Run-DMC.

Kings of Rock

Within weeks of the release of their first single, "It's Like That" in April 1983, the members of Run-DMC realized they had a winner on their hands. As more and more R&B radio stations in New York City and all over the country discovered the trailblazing record, sales of the 12-inch vinyl climbed steadily. Eventually, "It's Like That"/"Sucker MCs" sold 250,000 copies. Hip-hop fans loved the rousing beats and shouted, intertwined vocals in which Run and DMC, instead of merely trading off verses or complete lines like other rappers, alternated lyrics in the middle of a sentence or even a word. Heartened by the record's success, Jay, Run, and D—or DMC as he was now generally known—decided to take leaves of absence from college in order to focus on their music careers. As it turned out, none of the three would ever return to school.

When the executives at Profile Records saw the sale numbers "It's Like That"/"Sucker MCs" was generating, they rushed a second Run-DMC single into release: "Hard Times"/"Jam Master Jay." Cowritten by Russell Simmons a few years earlier, "Hard Times" painted a grim picture of economic despair in the inner city. Composed by DMC, the flip side of the 12-inch vinyl was a paean to the deejaying genius of Jay Mizell, or "Jam Master Jay," as he had recently renamed himself. Peaking at number 11 on *Billboard* magazine's Black Singles chart, by early 1984 Run-DMC's second single had sold more than 150,000 copies.

Eager to take advantage of the records' popularity, during the summer of 1983 Russell Simmons booked Run-DMC at scores of small nightclubs, roller rinks, and community events throughout the New York City area, sometimes lining up two or three gigs for the trio in a single evening. Although Run, Jay, and DMC did not earn a great deal of money from these performances, they provided the group with much-needed experience as well as a loyal fan base.

A NEW LOOK

Run-DMC's first appearance at a major hip-hop venue was at the Disco Fever in the South Bronx. Jam Master Jay missed the show because his ride never showed up. The group was still struggling to establish its own sense of style, and when DMC and Run made the mistake of showing up at the trendy dance club dressed in mock turtlenecks and checkered sports jackets, they were nearly laughed off the stage. Although the young audience was quickly won over by the rappers' clever wordplay, Run and D left Disco Fever that night feeling thoroughly humiliated. The two 19-year-olds turned for help to the most fashion-conscious member of their trio, 18-year-old Jay.

Run, DMC, and Jay *(above, left to right)* quickly became known for their signature look: black clothing, black fedoras and Kangol hats, thick gold chains, and Adidas without shoelaces.

Determined to stand out from the rest of the crowd, Jay had developed his own unique style as far back as the ninth grade. Throughout his high school years Jay's signature attire was a black velour hat accented with a feather, black-and-white shell-toed Adidas sneakers, and Lee jeans. Meticulous about details, he always made a point of coordinating the color of his shirt with his shoelaces. By the time he went off to college, the time and effort it required to change his shoelaces every day had led Jay to give up wearing them altogether. After all, he jokingly pointed out to Bill Adler, "It matches—no shoelaces matches with everything!"

After Run and D's fashion faux pas at Disco Fever, Jay—with the enthusiastic backing of Russell Simmons—persuaded the group to adopt a simple yet dramatic new look based largely on Jason's personal style. The group's much-imitated interpretation of "urban cool" included black velour fedora hats; black leather suits; unlaced, shell-toed Adidas; and large gold neck chains. The warm-weather version of what would in effect become Run-DMC's uniform for the next decade included a black terry-cloth Kangol hat instead of the fedora and an Adidas warm-up suit in place of the leather blazer and slacks.

The streamlined "street" look Jam Master Jay helped Run-DMC develop contrasted sharply with the fashion excesses of other contemporary rap artists. Glittering skin-tight pants, studded jackets, thigh-high boots, and flamboyant furs were the standard stage attire for Grand Master Flash, Kurtis Blow, and other early hip-hop stars. Years later, DMC would speculate that Run-DMC's unpretentious style of dress was a key factor in their growing popularity at the expense of older, more established rappers during the early 1980s: "We came dressed as is, and that's what made the fans relate to us more than any other rap bands because when they looked up on stage and saw us, it was like looking in a mirror," DMC mused.

AN ALBUM AND A VIDEO

By the end of 1983, sales of the group's singles remained strong, and Russell was booking the trio at some of New York City's hottest dance clubs and at more and more venues outside the city. Steve Plotnicki and Cory Robbins of Profile Records felt the time was right for Run-DMC to cut an album. The group headed for Greene Street Studio in Manhattan to record what is generally considered the first all-rap album.

Released in early 1984 and named simply *Run-DMC*, the group's debut album featured nine original songs, including the four tracks that had already been released as singles during the spring and summer of 1983. Among the most memorable of the new pieces was "Wake Up," Run-DMC's vision of a world without war, prejudice, or poverty, and the humorous "30 Days," with lyrics cowritten by Daniel Simmons, Run and Russell's father. The most innovative song on the album,

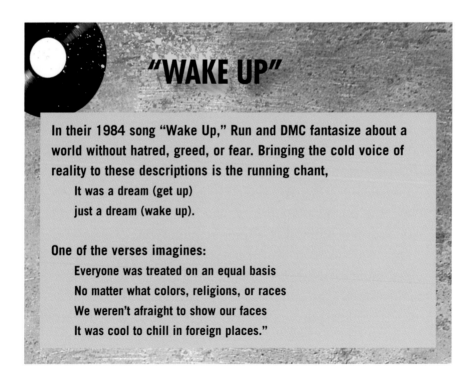

"WAKE UP"

In their 1984 song "Wake Up," Run and DMC fantasize about a world without hatred, greed, or fear. Bringing the cold voice of reality to these descriptions is the running chant,

> It was a dream (get up)
> just a dream (wake up).

One of the verses imagines:

> Everyone was treated on an equal basis
> No matter what colors, religions, or races
> We weren't afraight to show our faces
> It was cool to chill in foreign places."

however, was "Rock Box," a groundbreaking blend of heavy metal and rap that featured blaring guitar riffs by Eddie Martinez, a former bandmate of coproducer Larry Smith. "In their adventurous 'Rock Box,'" gushed music critic Debby Miller of *Rolling Stone* magazine, "Run and D.M.C. set their clipped, back-and-forth exchanges to a crying hard-rock guitar solo, melting rap into rock like it's never been done before."

An almost instant hit, *Run-DMC* eventually sold more than a half a million copies, making it the first rap album in history to go gold. An important factor in the album's impressive sales record was Run-DMC's hit music video of "Rock Box." The group's very first video also happened to be the first one by a rap group to be featured on MTV, which generally played few music videos by black artists during the early eighties. Costarring the popular comedian Professor Irwin Corey, the video was filmed at Danceteria, a trendy New York City nightclub, and showed Run-DMC rapping before an enthusiastic crowd of young fans, black and white, rockers and hip-hoppers alike. MTV played "Rock Box" on a regular rotation throughout mid-1984, bringing Run-DMC—and rap music in general—an unprecedented degree of national attention. Soon, the group was playing at bigger and more prestigious venues and being paid more money for their performances than ever before.

FRESH FEST

During the late spring of 1984, a young black concert promoter from Florida named Ricky Walker noted Run-DMC's growing national popularity with interest. In the past he had focused on R&B and rock groups, but an all hip-hop concert, Walker concluded, was a fresh idea with enormous commercial potential. Traveling to New York City, Walker met with Russell Simmons at Rush Productions, which now represented several popular New York rap artists in addition to Run-DMC.

Eager to gain as much national exposure as he could for his clients, Simmons was enthusiastic about Walker's plan.

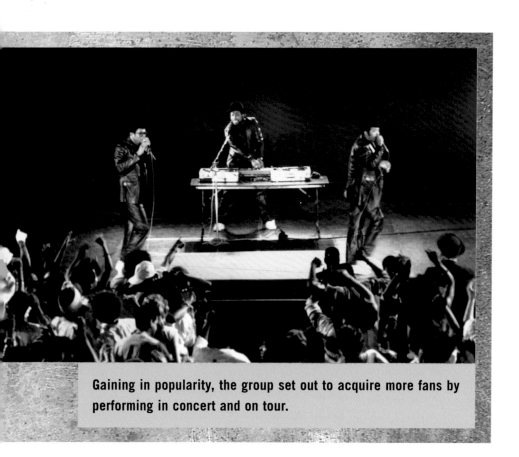

Gaining in popularity, the group set out to acquire more fans by performing in concert and on tour.

Simmons quickly persuaded his star rap acts to sign on for American's first-ever hip-hop concert tour—not only Run-DMC but also Kurtis Blow and Whodini, a trio from Brooklyn with several radio hits. Walker also recruited another well-known Brooklyn rap trio, the Fat Boys, and several break-dancing crews to entertain the audience between musical acts. Titled the Swatch Watch New York City Fresh Fest (Swatch was the sponsor), the tour was scheduled to play in more than 20 cities across the United States during the summer and autumn of 1984.

With Run-DMC at the top of the bill, the Fresh Fest tour was a resounding success, grossing $3.5 million during its almost four-month run. Yet as author Bill Adler points out in *Tougher Than Leather: The Rise of Run-DMC*:

> Fresh Fest was more than a moneymaker; it was a ground-breaker. It played in cities where *no* rap was played on the radio, like Chicago, and still sold ten thousand seats. In cities where they loved rap, like Philadelphia, the tour sold out the 19,000 seat Spectrum, quickly added a show, and sold another ten thousand seats in one day. . . . In sum, said Ricky Walker proudly, "The first Fresh Fest was like the pioneering of rock 'n' roll all over again, just like those barnstorming Alan Freed tours of the Fifties." And he was right. [Alan Freed was a radio personality and concert promoter who promoted African American R&B music during the fifties and is often credited for coining the term "Rock and Roll."]

KING OF ROCK AND *KRUSH GROOVE*

Toward the end of the Fresh Fest tour, Run-DMC began traveling back to New York City at the beginning of each week to record their second album, *King of Rock*. Russell Simmons and Larry Smith produced the album once again, but this time with the assistance of a new friend of Simmons's, a 21-year-old white college student and hip-hop enthusiast named Rick Rubin. By the time the album was finished, Simmons and Smith had parted ways, and Simmons had joined Rubin in founding a new record label specializing in hip-hop artists, Def Jam Recordings.

Although Run and the other members of Run-DMC wanted to sign with their manager's new label immediately, they couldn't because they were still under contract to Profile Records. Over the next few years, Simmons and Rubin's new company developed into one of the most successful labels in rap history with such popular artists as LL Cool J, Public Enemy, and the first all-white rap group, the Beastie Boys, on its roster.

A still from the 1985 musical film *Krush Groove* shows *(at right)* Jay and DMC listening to an audition. The group was excited to branch out into acting, though they didn't have to stretch much, since they played themselves. *Krush Groove* was not a mainstream hit, but it was financially successful and attracted a loyal audience of hip-hop fans. Now available on DVD, *Krush Groove* has become a cult hit.

Released by Profile in January 1985, *King of Rock* was an immediate hit with both the public and the critics, who particularly raved about the album's heavy-metal-infused title track in which DMC humorously boasts:

I'm the king of *rock*! There is none *higher*!
Sucker emcees should call me *sire*!
To burn my kingdom you must use *fire*!
I won't stop rockin' till I *retire*!"

A few weeks after the release of Run-DMC's second album, Simmons surprised the group by bringing them a contract for a movie deal. A 27-year-old film producer and Harlem native named George Jackson wanted to make a fictionalized account of Simmons's meteoric rise as a hip-hop promoter. He planned to cast a handsome young actor named Blair Underwood as Simmons and Simmons's star clients, including Run-DMC, LL Cool J, and the Beastie Boys, as themselves. Excited about the opportunity to try something entirely new, Run, DMC, and Jay quickly agreed to take part in the project, and filming began in early May 1985.

Krush Groove, as the movie was called, was completed in just 26 days on the slimmest of budgets. Shot almost entirely in Danceteria and the Bronx's Disco Fever, the film was blasted by the critics as a skimpily plotted vehicle for music videos by Run-DMC, LL Cool J, and the other rappers featured in the movie. Hip-hop fans, however, flocked to *Krush Groove*, which brought in over $3 million in ticket receipts during its first weekend alone.

By the end of 1985, Run, DMC, and Jay were unquestionably America's most famous hip-hop performers with numerous hit singles, two best-selling albums, a string of sold-out concert appearances, and a hit movie to their credit. Yet Run-DMC was more than just the most popular rap group in the United States; it was also the most influential. By the mid-eighties, Run-DMC's innovative and widely imitated style—their spare arrangements, driving rhythms, powerful lyrics, and right-off-the-street appearance—had changed the sound and look of rap forever.

"Walk This Way"

On July 13, 1985, the most celebrated rap group in America, Run-DMC, participated in the most celebrated rock benefit in history, Live Aid. Organized by Irish rock guitarist and humanitarian Bob Geldof, the giant event featured two concerts held simultaneously in Philadelphia's JFK Stadium and London's Wembley Stadium. Sixty different acts played at the two venues, with Run-DMC—who performed at JFK—being the only rappers on the entire lineup. Attended by an estimated 160,000 people, the concerts were broadcast to some one billion television viewers across the globe. Thanks to Run-DMC, Madonna, Paul McCartney, Tina Turner, and the other music superstars who took part in the event, the 16-hour-long fund-raiser was a resounding success, raising

On July 13, 1985, Run-DMC hit the stage at JFK Stadium in Philadelphia as part of the massive benefit Live Aid. The concert occurred simultaneously in Philadelphia and London and featured more than 52 acts performing in the name of famine relief. Run-DMC were the only rappers to be included in the legendary event.

more than $120 million to assist the famine-stricken population of Ethiopia in East Africa.

Within a few months of the Live Aid concert event, Run, DMC, and Jay were once again donating their talents to a worthy cause. This time around their focus was apartheid, a notorious policy of racial discrimination and segregation enforced by the white-minority government of South Africa from the late 1940s until the mid-1990s. Appalled by South Africa's racist and repressive political system, the trio agreed to contribute to *Sun City*, an antiapartheid record being produced by American rock musician and political activist "Little" Steven Van Zandt. For Van Zandt and many of apartheid's other opponents during the 1980s, Sun City, a luxurious resort that catered to wealthy whites yet was set in an impoverished, overwhelmingly black region of South Africa, was a symbol of the country's blatantly discriminatory policies. Hoping to reach as wide an audience as possible, Van Zandt invited a remarkably diverse group of performers to take part in his musical protest against Sun City and apartheid, ranging from rockers Bruce Springsteen and Keith Richards to jazz legends Miles Davis and Herbie Hancock to rappers Run-DMC and the Fat Boys. All profits from the sale of *Sun City*, went to the Africa Fund, which provided financial and other forms of assistance to South African political prisoners and their families.

In December 1985, Run-DMC finished off the year by contributing to another all-star benefit record: a musical salute to the slain civil rights activist Martin Luther King Jr. (1929–1968) entitled "King Holiday." Released shortly before the first national observance of Martin Luther King Day on January 15, 1986, the partly rapped, partly sung single was meant to teach young Americans about Dr. King's life and philosophy. Coproduced by the late reverend's youngest son, Dexter Scott King and rapper Kurtis Blow, "King Holiday" eventually climbed to number 30 on the R&B chart.

RAISING HELL

During the winter of 1986, the three members of Run-DMC turned their attention to a new album, which they dubbed *Raising Hell*. Determined to make all of their own creative decisions this time around, Run, DMC, and Jay produced their third album with only minimal input from their manager and previous producer, Russell Simmons, and his new partner Rick Rubin.

Destined to be Run-DMC's most popular album ever, within just five weeks of its release in the summer of 1986, *Raising Hell* had already sold one million copies and been certified platinum—an unprecedented accomplishment for a rap album. By early autumn, the LP had climbed to number one on the R&B charts—another first for a hip-hop album. When *Raising Hell* later peaked at number three on the U.S. pop charts, it became the first rap album ever to break into the *Billboard* Top 10.

The album also achieved one more "first" when it was nominated for a Grammy in 1986—the first Grammy nomination ever for a rap album or group. The nomination was for Best R&B Vocal Performance by a Duo or Group because a Grammy category for rap did not yet exist. (Run-DMC lost to Prince at the 29th Grammy Awards held in early 1987.)

Much of *Raising Hell's* phenomenal success can be traced to the smash hit single that it spawned, a cover of the rock classic "Walk This Way" by the hard-rock group Aerosmith. Recorded with Aerosmith's lead singer and lead guitarist, Steven Tyler and Joe Perry, "Walk This Way's" energetic blending of rap and hard rock brought Run-DMC—and hip-hop in general—its first mainstream hit single. Rapidly climbing to number four on the *Billboard* Top 10 singles chart, "Walk This Way" also gave rise to a popular music video featuring Tyler, Perry, and Run-DMC performing the song onstage before a theater full of screaming rock and hip-hop fans.

Raising Hell generated several other top-selling singles for the group, including "My Adidas," "It's Tricky," and the humorous "You Be Illin'." "My Adidas," Run and D's ode to their favorite sneakers, also helped land Run-DMC a lucrative and groundbreaking endorsement deal with the German sportswear manufacturer. The first non-athletes ever to be offered an endorsement contract by Adidas, Run, Jay, and DMC reportedly received $1.5 million for lending their name to a new line of sneakers. Packaged in a special black box emblazoned with

Run-DMC's 1986 collaboration with rock band Aerosmith on a rap version of that group's smash hit "Walk This Way" brought them closer to the mainstream and heavy rotation on MTV. Here, Aerosmith lead singer Steven Tyler appears at the 2002 Billboard Music Awards with DMC.

the group's red and white logo instead of Adidas's customary blue-and-white striped box, the Run-DMC athletic shoes featured the rounded shell toes that the trio had long favored.

TROUBLE AT LONG BEACH

In late May 1986, Run-DMC embarked on a highly publicized national tour to promote their newest album. The Raising Hell Tour also featured three of Russell Simmons's other big rap acts—LL Cool J, Whodini, and the Beastie Boys. Throughout the summer of 1986, Run-DMC and their fellow rappers performed before sold-out crowds in New York City, Philadelphia, Cleveland, and a host of other major American cities. Then on August 17 at the Long Beach Arena just outside Los Angeles, the tour ran into trouble.

Upward of 14,000 rap fans showed up at the arena that August evening along with hundreds of members of rival street gangs from the greater Los Angeles area. It quickly became evident that the gangsters had not come to Long Beach for the music—they had come for a showdown. Even before Run-DMC had a chance to go on stage, intergang fights had broken out on the floor of the packed auditorium. Soon the brawlers were breaking the metal legs off the arena's chairs and using

"PROUD TO BE BLACK"

For their album, *Raising Hell,* Run and DMC wanted to include a song that addressed the issue of race, and particularly the experiences of blacks, in America. The result was "Proud to Be Black," which they cowrote with Andre "Dr. Dre" Brown. Following are some lines from the song:

> I ain't no slave, I ain't bailing no hay
> We're in a tight position, in any condition
> Don't get in my way, 'cause I'm full of ambition
> I'm proud to be black, and I ain't taking no crap.

them to club not only each other but also innocent bystanders. "It was like a stampede—chairs coming up in the air, panicked kids in the crowd, knowing the gangs were coming their way and couldn't get out," Run later told Bill Adler. "You could see 300 people all moving against one section, beating and robbing them. I was really scared for our fans out there."

As more and more gang members began to push their way to the front of the auditorium, the arena's overwhelmed security guards finally persuaded Run, DMC, Jam Master Jay, and the other horrified performers watching the mayhem from backstage to barricade themselves in a dressing room. Run-DMC and the rest of the musicians stayed there for more than two hours until 60 Los Angeles policemen in full riot gear finally arrived on the scene about 11:00 P.M. Within 15 minutes, the baton-wielding police had cleared out the bloodstained and vandalized arena. Forty-five concertgoers were sent to local hospitals, several with life-threatening injuries.

Run-DMC Under Fire

Back at their hotel Jay, Run, and DMC listened to televised accounts of the riot in disbelief. Instead of blaming intergang rivalries for the bloodshed at the arena, the local newscasters were blaming rap music, which they said encouraged violence and disrespect for authority. By morning, the national media had picked up the story and were also accusing the stars of the Raising Hell Tour—and especially the tour's headliners, Run-DMC—of inciting the riot through their allegedly violent and inflammatory lyrics. During the next days and weeks, the trio was compelled repeatedly to defend not only their good name, "but rap music itself," DMC would later recall in *King of Rock*. In one interview after another, the group urged their critics to scrutinize the lyrics of their songs for anything that could possibly incite listeners to violence.

No matter what the news media said about them, Run-DMC's fans remained fiercely loyal to the group. Although a

Darryl McDaniels and Jason Mizell hold a press conference to discuss the tragic riot that occurred during their Long Beach, California, concert in 1986. Although the band was unfairly blamed for the riots, McDaniels and Mizell announced they would not play another area concert until the police could guarantee the safety of their fans.

handful of their concerts in Los Angeles and other American cities were cancelled by promoters or municipal officials worried about security, for the most part the Raising Hell Tour went on as scheduled before large, enthusiastic—and generally peaceful—audiences. In early autumn, as the tour was winding down, the trio became the first rappers to be asked to pose for the cover of *Rolling Stone*, America's leading rock music magazine. Still sensitive about the negative publicity that the Long Beach incident had generated, the group invited *Rolling Stone* writer

Ed Kiersh to accompany them to a special appearance at a Los Angeles radio station in early October, where the group blasted gang violence and once again denied that their music—or rap generally—was in any way responsible for the riot in August.

By the end of 1986, the Long Beach controversy had blown over and the members of Run-DMC found themselves in higher demand than ever before. After completing a sold-out tour of Japan, Run, DMC, and Jay were invited to appear on several popular television shows, including the hit comedy sketch program *Saturday Night Live.* With their new line of Adidas footwear about to hit the stores and their last album, *Raising Hell,* well on its way to achieving triple-platinum status, the future looked bright for the three young men from Hollis, Queens.

Down with the King

In early 1987, Run-DMC began filming their second feature film, *Tougher Than Leather*. Cowritten by their publicist, Bill Adler, and directed by Russell Simmons's business partner, Rick Rubin, the group's new movie was intended to be a parody of the popular blaxploitation films of the early 1970s such as *Shaft* and *Superfly*. Typically set in the ghetto and featuring exaggerated violence and sexuality, blaxploitation movies were targeted at inner-city audiences and starred African-American actors. In Run-DMC's updated version of the film genre, Run, DMC, and Jam Master Jay played a streetwise rap group whose friend is murdered by a drug lord posing as a music promoter (played by Rick Rubin). By the end of the 95-minute-long movie, the trio has tracked down and brutally killed the evil drug boss, beaten up some rednecks, and performed several new rap numbers.

Although disappointed in the amateurish quality of the script, Run, DMC, and Jay clung to the hope that *Tougher Than Leather* would be a box-office hit like *Krush Groove*, especially since they had poured hundreds of thousands of their own earnings into making the movie. But when the film was finally released during the summer of 1988, the reviews were scathing, and the ticket-buying public stayed away in droves. Richard Harrington of the *Washington Post* blasted the low-budget film as

> vile, vicious, despicable, stupid . . . and horrendously made. *[Tougher Than Leather]* could have been an opportunity to say something about hip-hop culture, about the environ-ment that bred it, about the energies that fuel it. Instead it's just the crassest exploitation. Had the film been made by professionals but with the same script, it would have been bad enough, but this crew sinks to the occasion at every level. Save your money and wait for it to come out on video. Then skip it again.

Around the same time that the film *Tougher Than Leather* was bombing in the movie theaters, Run-DMC released a fourth album by the same name. The album proved to be another bitter disappointment for Run, DMC, and Jay. The new LP spawned two modest hits, "Run's House" and "Mary Mary," a cover of a song by the sixties pop group the Monkees. Despite the fact that the album eventually went platinum, to the group's dismay, *Tougher Than Leather* never came close to matching the extraordinary commercial success of *Raising Hell* and its monster hit single, "Walk This Way." Nor did the album garner the rave reviews that *Raising Hell* had enjoyed for its innovative fusion of rock and rap. Although critics were generally enthusiastic about the hard-driving beats and

Hoping to continue their movie career, Russell Simmons and Rick Rubin again teamed up on the feature *Tougher Than Leather*. Run-DMC starred in the film and helped finance it, making its failure especially hard to take. Here, Jam Master Jay, Rick Rubin, Run, and DMC wait for cinematographer Feliks Parnell to set up the shot.

swaggering rhymes of such tracks as "Run's House" and "I'm Not Going Out Like That," many reviewers thought that the album as a whole lacked the freshness and energy of Run-DMC's previous work.

RUN-DMC AND THE CHANGING WORLD OF RAP

Because of a contractual dispute between Run-DMC and their label, Profile Records, *Tougher Than Leather* did not reach the stores until more than six months after its completion.

Seminal group Public Enemy—including members Flavor Flav and Chuck D *(above)*—burst on the hip-hop scene with their 1987 debut album *Yo! Bum Rush the Show* and aggressively changed the course of rap music. With their politically charged lyrics and innovative techniques, PE suddenly raised the bar for the hip-hop form, making some early rappers seem safe and irrelevant.

Consequently, two entire years passed between the release of Run-DMC's third and fourth albums. The feud between Run-DMC and Profile, noted David Thigpen in *Jam Master Jay,* came at "the worst possible time: The blockbuster success of *Raising Hell* had raised expectations among its growing fan base for a quick follow-up." But the lengthy delay in releasing *Tougher Than Leather* did more harm to Run-DMC than merely causing frustration among the group's fans. It also meant that the album struck many listeners as out of date. During the late eighties, the sound and style of rap was changing at a remarkably rapid pace. Consequently, by the time it hit the stores, *Tougher Than Leather* was already out of sync with much of the rest of hip-hop. Just a few years earlier, Run-DMC had revolutionized the sound of rap with their spare arrangements, clever back-and-forth wordplay, and blaring heavy-metal riffs, leaving "old school" rappers and their disco party–inspired music in the dust. Now Run, DMC, and Jam Master Jay were being pushed aside by trailblazing new groups like political rappers Public Enemy and "gangsta" rappers N.W.A.

By 1988 when *Tougher Than Leather* was finally released, the rap world had become highly politicized. By far the most popular and influential of the new political rappers was the black nationalist group Public Enemy, whose militant album, *It Takes a Nation of Millions to Hold Us Back,* was a huge hit with critics and the record-buying public alike. Compared to Public Enemy's searing indictments of a racist and uncaring American government and media, some critics thought Run-DMC's "message" songs about poverty or bigotry, such as their 1983 hit "It's Like That" or "Proud to Be Black" from *Raising Hell,* seemed rather mild. Moreover, with the exception of the anticrime track "I'm Not Going Out Like That," Run and DMC all but ignored serious social and political issues in the lyrics they created for *Tougher Than Leather.*

As hardcore political rap was transforming hip-hop music during the late 1980s, another form of rap that was destined to have an even greater impact on the genre was also rapidly gaining popularity: "gangsta" rap. Whereas Run-DMC and most of the other leading rap acts of the early to mid-eighties had generally steered clear of violent or sexually explicit lyrics, gangsta rappers like the Los Angeles group N.W.A. focused almost exclusively on the darker side of inner-city America. In 1988, N.W.A.'s blockbuster album, *Straight Outta Compton,* celebrated the illegal drug use, promiscuous sex, and street warfare associated with the outlaw or gangsta lifestyle. Many people were outraged by the woman-bashing, police-baiting, gun-glorifying album, and the FBI and a number of other private and governmental organizations called for censorship of gangsta rap's more offensive or inflammatory lyrics. Yet the widespread outcry against N.W.A.'s troubling lyrics did nothing to hinder the group's burgeoning popularity. Indeed, if anything, the criticism only seemed to make the rebellious rap group and the legion of gangsta imitators who followed in their wake all the more attractive to many young Americans, white and black alike.

BACK FROM HELL

By 1990, blockbuster albums by gangsta rappers N.W.A., Ice Cube, and Luther Campbell were racing up the charts, and gangsta rap was well on its way to becoming the most commercially lucrative style of hip-hop in the United States. Discouraged by *Tougher Than Leather's* lackluster sales, Run, DMC, and Jay took a stab at the controversial new rap subgenre on their fifth album, *Back from Hell*. In his autobiography, *King of Rock*, DMC described the group's decision to try to jump-start their careers by "going gangster" on *Back from Hell*:

> We tried to curse, we're talking about . . . ho's, getting high, drinking, smacking people with the back of a gun. It was the height of gangsta rap, when N.W.A. and Luther Campbell made violence and sex the flavor of the moment. We made that album out of desperation because we realized our sales were going down, that our appeal was waning. It seemed like it wouldn't be that long before nobody wanted to hear us. Our career slump had also affected our live shows, which provided a good deal of our cash flow. We weren't getting as many shows, and the ones we did weren't paying as much as before. So we made the choice. We said, "All right, we're

going to go make a record that sounds like what the people apparently want to hear."

When the album was released in the autumn of 1990, however, it quickly became evident that Run-DMC had made a grave miscalculation. "The album flopped," DMC explained in *King of Rock*. "It might have been what people wanted to hear, but it wasn't what they wanted to hear from us. And because our hearts weren't really in it, it showed. We knew that gangsta wasn't really us, and so did our fans."

By the start of 1991, *Back from Hell* had failed to sell even 500,000 copies. Although the bad language and violent imagery on the album were tame compared to what Ice Cube, N.W.A., or other blockbuster gangsta acts were then including on their albums, Run-DMC's fans were clearly put off by the group's angry lyrics and thuggish stance. "One big part of Run-DMC's success was our catchy rhymes that made you think or sometimes laugh: No violence or harsh language, just thinking, laughing, and having fun," Run noted years later in his autobiography, *It's Like That*. "Struggling to appear relevant next to Ice Cube and the Geto Boys," Mark Coleman of *Rolling Stone* would note bluntly in his January 1991 review of *Back from Hell*, "Run-D.M.C. has shot itself in the foot."

TOUGH TIMES FOR RUN AND DMC

After what Run-DMC had hoped would be their comeback album flopped, the group's founders, Run and DMC, went through a particularly difficult period, personally as well as professionally. Convinced that the group would never regain its past glory, Run became chronically depressed. Turning to drugs for solace, he began smoking up to six bags of marijuana a day. Then in August 1991, while the group was on tour in Cleveland, Ohio, a college student accused Run of sexually assaulting her in his hotel room after a concert. Although the judge threw the

REV RUN ON REINVENTING YOURSELF

In his book, *It's Like That: A Spiritual Memoir,* Run gives his readers advice regarding how to overcome disappointments and setbacks and move forward with life, advice based on his own experiences in regaining his confidence and drive after the fortunes of Run-DMC began to decline in the late 1980s and early 1990s:

You have a mission in life whether you know it or not. Don't let obstacles hold you back; *you* hold you back! Problems are really opportunities for self-improvement. Learn from your mistakes, meditate, make changes, and move forward. . .

IT'S LIKE THIS . . .

- It's never too late to reinvent yourself. And it's always in your power to do so. . . .
- You can only beat yourself. You can only take your *own* light.
- You have to know that there's a new you inside if you ever want to be able to find it. . . .
- It's not all about you . . . so stop thinking it is. . . .

Reinventing yourself means realizing that at your core is a valuable treasure. Years of dirt may be heaped on top of that treasure, so you may have never seen it. . . . It's the gift from God that we all have within us whether we know it—or remember it—or not. I think of it as a diamond. . . . Uncovering that diamond is the reinventing yourself process. You first have to be able to see the new you in your mind's eye. . . . Problems occur to help direct you in life. Sometimes we only learn the value of something by losing it. Never believe it is over. I lost everything. My self-esteem was low, my vision clouded. But, deep inside, I knew that if I hung in there long enough and kept the faith I could make a comeback.

case out of court on the first day of the trial in February 1992, by that point Run had used up most of his savings hiring a defense team.

Soon after the case was dismissed, Run's already shaky marriage to his former high school sweetheart, Valerie, completely disintegrated. Run's depression deepened to the point that he even contemplated suicide. "I had no—absolutely no—thoughts of going forward with life," Run recalled years later in *It's Like That.* "People said, 'Get up and fight, Run,' but I didn't want to get up and fight. I was hurt. I wanted to lie down and die!"

While Run was struggling to cope with severe depression, DMC was also going through tough times. Naturally shy, DMC had been relying on alcohol to help him overcome his debilitating stage fright ever since he had gotten drunk on whisky before his first public appearance at a Hollis nightclub when he was 16 years old. As the group's fortunes declined after 1988, DMC began drinking more and more, downing as many as 12 40-ounce bottles of malt liquor a day. Finally, after waking up one morning with a stabbing pain in his abdomen, DMC was rushed to the hospital where doctors diagnosed acute pancreatitis. His pancreas, the organ that plays a critical role in breaking down food as it travels through the digestive system, had become dangerously inflamed by the huge amounts of alcohol that he was consuming. Told he must either give up alcohol for good or die, DMC embarked on a long and difficult journey to sobriety.

Jay was the only member of the trio whose personal and professional life remained relatively stable during the late eighties and early nineties as Run-DMC's popularity began to wane. One of the best-known and respected DJs in the world, he had no trouble securing high-paying gigs at dance clubs, parties, and conventions all over the United States and Europe. Jay also became involved in record production, and in 1991, he launched his own hip-hop label, Jam Master Jay.

Professional disappointments, the end of his marriage, and debts drove Run into a deep depression. His Christian faith brought him out, and eventually he became an ordained minister. Today he refers to himself as "Rev Run."

DOWN WITH THE KING

By 1993, Run and DMC had overcome their addictions to marijuana and alcohol and committed themselves anew to the Christian faith in which they had been raised. After hearing about a nondenominational Manhattan church from one of Run's bodyguards, both men joined Zoe Ministries, headed by the televangelist Bishop E. Bernard Jordan. Soon Run was ordained as a pastor in Zoe Ministries and adopted Rev Run as his new stage name. As Run's involvement in Zoe Ministries deepened, however, DMC was gradually drifting away from the church and organized religion in general. Yet he did not lose his newfound interest in spiritual matters. A voracious reader, DMC drew spiritual strength and moral guidance from Buddhist and Islamic texts as well as the Bible and works by Christian theologians.

Run and DMC announced their religious awakenings to the world on their sixth album, *Down with the King*, released in May 1993. Featuring guest appearances by hip-hop stars Public Enemy, Pete Rock, and Q Tip, the album eventually went gold and spawned a top 10 single (also named "Down with the King"). Reviews of the album, and particularly of the title track, in which Run and DMC rap about their spiritual faith, were positive. It seemed that Run, DMC, and Jam Master Jay were finally on the verge of their long-hoped-for comeback.

New Directions

Despite the success of *Down with the King*, it was six years before Run-DMC began recording another album. Contributing to the group's lengthy hiatus between records was the fact that Profile, their longtime label, was bought out by another record company, Arista, in the mid-nineties. Preoccupied with their roster's top-selling artists, Arista's executives displayed little interest in a new recording project by Run-DMC. Around the same time that Arista acquired Profile, the group was faced with another even more daunting challenge: After years of overuse, DMC was losing his voice.

By 1997, DMC's once booming shout had been reduced to little more than a hoarse whisper. At first baffled by DMC's

HIP-HOP GOES MAINSTREAM

In his biography of Jay Mizell, *Jam Master Jay: The Heart of Hip-Hop,* journalist David E. Thigpen described the influence and growing mainstream popularity of hip-hop music and culture during the late twentieth and early twenty-first centuries:

> After jazz music, hip-hop music became America's second great original art form. Although there are plenty of social critics and politicians who do not concede the "art" part of that equation, they need only look at the music that is thriving beneath the purview of the popular press. They'll find that hip-hop's conscience and humanity and highly skilled wordplay and musicianship do exist in a variety of places: in the thought-provoking songs of the Brooklyn rapper Talib Kweli, in the uplift and social conscience of the Chicago rapper Common, or in the acute political critiques of Oakland's Michael Franti and Philadelphia's The Roots.
>
> By the early 1990s rap was a gigantic industry and before 2000 arrived it would be well along in its crossover into the cultural and commercial mainstream. Baggy pants, athletic jerseys, unlaced sneakers, even the styles of speech coined by rappers were picked up and copied by kids of all economic classes and all races. By 1998 some 80 percent of the hip-hop records sold in the United States were bought by whites. Barely four years later hip-hop sales would tally a staggering $5 billion and help the record industry to strong profits when genres such as alternative rock and R&B were slowing down.

voice problems, doctors finally diagnosed spasmodic dysphonia, a neurological disorder in which one or more muscles of the larynx (voice box) go into involuntary spasms. Years of screaming lyrics in concerts and on recordings had taken a heavy toll on the 33-year-old's vocal cords. Even with vocal coaching and medical treatment, it soon became evident that DMC's powerful baritone was gone forever, and his rapping would never be the same again.

CROWN ROYAL

In 1998, Run-DMC received an unexpected boon when a New York DJ named Jason Nevins recorded a remix of their very first hit, "It's Like That," that quickly sold four million copies. The group's touring, which had continued throughout the decade despite their dearth of new recordings, was reenergized, and for the first time in years Jay, Run, and DMC were being booked at 3,000–5000 seat auditoriums in the United States and Europe. By 1999, the group had made it back to the studio at last to record their seventh album, *Crown Royal,* for a newly enthusiastic Arista Records.

Unfortunately for the group, the long-awaited recording sessions for *Crown Royal* did not go smoothly. Still plagued by voice problems, DMC ended up performing on only three songs. DMC had repeatedly urged Run to move away from the aggressive, hard-rock-influenced rapping style of the group's past toward a softer style better suited to his fragile vocal cords. Hesitant to abandon Run-DMC's signature sound, Run obstinately refused, and DMC finally walked out of the recording studio for good. To make up for DMC's absence—and in hopes of appealing to a younger audience—Run and Jay relied heavily on guest artists in making *Crown Royal,* including popular rocker-rappers Sugar Ray and Kid Rock.

Following a series of frustrating delays, *Crown Royal* was finally released in early 2001. Sales of the new CD were lackluster, however. Fans and music critics alike were dismayed by DMC's minimal role in the recording and unimpressed by Run and Jay's collaborations with Kid Rock and the other guest stars. In the wake of *Crown Royal*'s disheartening reception by the public and music critics alike, DMC made his peace with Run and Jay, and the group went back to touring, mostly performing at colleges and smaller auditoriums in the United States.

A COMEBACK AND A TRAGIC DEATH

After a disappointing 2001, the year 2002 started out exceptionally well for the group. Nearly two decades after the trio had first formed, it seemed that Run-DMC had at last attained the status of respected elders of rap. On February 25, Run, Jay, and DMC traveled to California to set their handprints in cement on the RockWalk on Sunset Boulevard in Hollywood, California. A large crowd, including rap stars Jay-Z and Snoop Dogg, applauded as Run-DMC became the first hip-hop artists ever to be awarded this honor. Two weeks later, the threesome was inducted into the brand new Hip-Hop Hall of Fame in New York City along with DJ Kool Herc, Afrika Bambaataa, and a dozen of hip-hop's other most influential rappers and DJs from the past quarter century.

Soon after the ceremony, Aerosmith, Run-DMC's hard-rock collaborators on "Walk This Way," invited the group to join them and Kid Rock on a tour that included more than 40 shows in major venues across the United States that summer and autumn. Jay and Run did their best to cover for DMC's still unreliable voice and throughout the sold-out, cross-country tour, the group was greeted with wild ovations whenever they stepped on stage. Bolstered by their warm reception, the trio discussed making a new album to mark their upcoming twentieth anniversary as a group.

Then, on the night of Wednesday, October 30, 2002, the unthinkable happened: 37-year-old Jam Master Jay was shot dead in his Queens recording studio by an unidentified gunman.

February 25, 2002, was a proud day for the members of Run-DMC. The three artists were inducted into the Hollywood RockWalk at the Guitar Center in Hollywood, California. The Rockwalk prides itself on its standards: Inductees are chosen solely by past honorees, not by the public.

Darryl McDaniels flashes the peace sign to spectators on his way to the funeral of his friend and band mate Jam Master Jay on November 5, 2002. Mizell was eulogized by Run and DMC to a crowd of hip-hop luminaries.

Almost immediately rumors started to circulate that Jay had been killed because of an unpaid debt or a cocaine deal gone wrong. Some people even speculated that Jay's execution-style murder was meant as a message to his young protégé, the popular rapper 50 Cent, a former Queens drug dealer who was reputed to have many enemies.

Infuriated by the speculation regarding Jay's death and particularly by tabloid stories that portrayed him as a gangster, Jay's bandmates and the hip-hop community in general rushed to his defense. Jay was a peace-loving family man, they said,

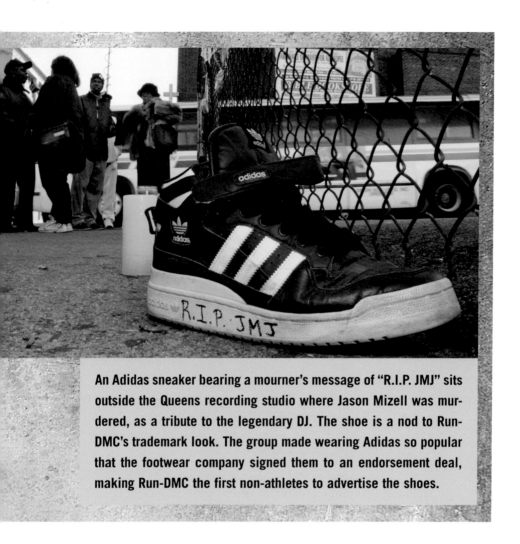

An Adidas sneaker bearing a mourner's message of "R.I.P. JMJ" sits outside the Queens recording studio where Jason Mizell was murdered, as a tribute to the legendary DJ. The shoe is a nod to Run-DMC's trademark look. The group made wearing Adidas so popular that the footwear company signed them to an endorsement deal, making Run-DMC the first non-athletes to advertise the shoes.

utterly devoted to his wife of 11 years, Terri, and his three children. Run and DMC remembered Jay as one of the kindest and most unselfish individuals they had ever known, a man whose personal character was as outstanding as his deejaying skills. Resolved to give back to his community, Jay chose to live in a modest house in his hometown of Hollis. Jay's commitment to serving as a role model and mentor to the younger generation was legendary in Queens: He regularly lent out his Merrick Avenue recording studio to aspiring local musicians free of charge, and on Saturday afternoons when he was not touring,

Jay could often be found at a neighborhood park teaching kids how to play chess or basketball.

On November 5, six days after Jay's murder, nearly 2,500 mourners, including such hip-hop luminaries of the past and present as Grandmaster Flash, the Beastie Boys, LL Cool J, and Queen Latifah, attended a funeral service for the slain DJ at the Greater Allen African Methodist Episcopal Cathedral in Queens. DMC brought the congregation to their feet when he rapped from his 1983 ode to Jay, "Jam Master Jay":

> Jam Master Jay, that is his name
> And all the wild DJs he will tame . . .
> So when asked who's the best, ya'll should say
> 'Jason Mizell, Jam Master Jay!'"

Then, after leading the mourners in prayer, Run eulogized his friend and bandmate with a mingling of admiration and affection. "He helped to create this hip-hop nation," Run told his listeners. "Jason walked in grace, in style, and with class."

RUN AND DMC ON THEIR OWN

Within days of Jay's funeral, Run and DMC officially disbanded Run-DMC. After all the years that the group performed together, Run could not bring himself to get out in front of Run-DMC's fans with a new DJ, he explained to mourners and members of the press at a news conference. "I don't know any other way but with the three original members," he said.

Aside from their participation in memorials and tributes to Jason Mizell, Run and DMC stayed out of the public eye for more than two years after the announcement of Run-DMC's retirement. Then in 2005, Run began shooting a reality show for MTV entitled *Run's House* based on the day-to-day lives of his family, including his five children and second wife, Justine. Produced by Russell Simmons and hip-hop mogul Sean "P. Diddy" Combs, the humorous yet often thought-provoking

Run has successfully jumped on the reality show bandwagon with his MTV hit, *Run's House*. The show follows Rev Run and his family in their chaotic New Jersey home. To promote the show, Run and his family appeared at the MTV Times Square studios for this December 19, 2005 portrait. From left are JoJo, Run, Justine, Russy, Angela, Vanessa, and Diggy.

show attracted a loyal audience and was quickly renewed for the 2006–2007 season.

Toward the end of the second season of "Run's House," the Simmons family received the exciting news that 43-year-old Justine was pregnant. The program's third season was supposed to be launched in April 2007 with the birth of Justine and Run's new daughter, Victoria Anne Simmons. The infant suffered from a grave birth defect known as omphalocele, which caused her organs to develop outside of her body.

Run and Justine became aware of the baby's condition about half way through the pregnancy. However, the couple, who for religious reasons did not consider abortion as an option, decided to tell no one about the baby's medical problems except for their pastor, Bishop Jordan. "Our faith told us that God could give us a miracle and this baby could be born with no problems," Justine later explained to *Newsweek* magazine. Sadly, less than two hours after her delivery, tiny Victoria died at a New Jersey hospital. MTV's cameras caught the stunned and heartbroken reactions of Justine and Run's other five children when they heard the news about their sister.

The Simmonses' decision to allow the footage to be aired on national television was controversial; the show drew more than 3.4 million viewers and some critics suggested that the program's producers were trying to exploit the tragedy. Run, however, strongly defended the decision to keep the television cameras rolling that day, declaring: "I may be famous, I may have bling, but tragedy comes to my door just as it does

EXCERPTS FROM "JUST LIKE ME" BY DARRYL MCDANIELS

It was 9 whole months inside of the womb
Another long month in the hospital room
Facin doom in a tomb cause the kid is alone
But somebody came along and they took the kid home
He came into the world like we all do
But he never ever knew how he came through
Do the best you can do if this happen to you
And understand all the words that I'm rappin to you

anybody's else's. That's a message that cannot be pressed hard enough when celebrities are so much on a pedestal."

Around the time that *Run's House* premiered in the autumn of 2005, Rev Run also released his first solo album, *Distortion,* on his older brother's new record label, Russell Simmons Music Group. On the album, Run raps about such diverse topics as urban poverty, teenage pregnancy, and his own spiritual rebirth. He also pays tribute to Jason Mizell in the rock-rap song "Home Sweet Home."

Several months after the album's release, Run, who authored an autobiography, *It's Like That: A Spiritual Memoir,* in 2000, published his second book, a collection of inspirational thoughts entitled, *Words of Wisdom: Daily Affirmations of Faith.* In the book Run advises his readers: "All great blessings come from being at peace.... Work hard and let God do the rest. I always say these words at night: 'I can sleep tonight because God is awake!'"

In March 2006, DMC released his first solo album, *Checks, Thugs & Rock N Roll.* The album includes an emotional farewell to Jam Master Jay as well as appearances by a number of guest artists including Rev Run, Aerosmith, Kid Rock, and pop-folk star Sarah McLachlan, whose song "Angel" helped lift DMC out of a deep depression in the late 1990s. McLachlan sings on the chorus of "Just Like Me," a poignant track inspired by DMC's stunning discovery six years earlier at age 35 that he had been adopted as an infant. A month before DMC's solo album was released, the cable television network VH1 aired a documentary based on DMC's long search for and ultimate reunion with his birth mother, Berncenia Lovelace of Staten Island, New York.

Inspired by his own experience to serve as an advocate for orphaned and abandoned children, in February 2006, McDaniels and casting director Sheila Jaffe, another adoptee who had recently reunited with her birth parents, co-founded the Felix Organization/Adoptees for Children. The organization's mission was to provide new and enriching opportunities

Although, sadly, Run-DMC will never perform again, they will be remembered for their many contributions to music. The commercially-successful and critically-acclaimed rappers (here at the 31st Annual Grammy Awards in 1988) influenced scores of musicians in all genres.

and experiences for parentless children. To that end McDaniels and Jaffee founded a summer camp, Camp Felix, in Putnam Valley, New York. During the summer of 2006, the Felix Organization sent 150 foster children to the camp for one week each, where they enjoyed such activities as swimming, softball, and arts and crafts. For his efforts in trying to create better lives for children in foster care, in December 2006 DMC was honored by the Congressional Coalition on Adoption Institute at their annual National Angels in Adoption Gala in Washington D.C.

Run-DMC's groundbreaking style, including their minimalist musical arrangements, edgy yet literate lyrics, melding of rap with rock and roll, and straight-off-the-street look, transformed hip-hop during the first half of the 1980s. In the process, Jason "Jam Master Jay" Mizell, Joseph "Run" Simmons, and Darryl "DMC" McDaniels brought the New York City-born movement unprecedented national attention and acceptance. Although Run-DMC was officially disbanded in 2002, the groundbreaking contributions of the three young men from Hollis, Queens, to the evolution of rap ensure that their place in the history of hip-hop music and culture will remain forever secure.

DISCOGRAPHY

Run-D.M.C. (1984)

King of Rock (1985)

Raising Hell (1986)

Tougher Than Leather (1988)

Back from Hell (1990)

Together Forever: Greatest Hits 1983–1991 (1991)

Down with the King (1993)

Crown Royal (1999)

High Profile: Original Rhymes (2002)

Greatest Hits (2002)

Best of Run-DMC (2003)

Ultimate Run-DMC (2003)

Artist Collection: Run DMC (2004)

Distortion (2005), Rev Run

Checks, Thugs & Rock N Roll (2006), DMC

1957 **October 4** Russell Simmons born in Queens, New York.

1964 **May 31** Darryl "DMC" McDaniels born in the Harlem neighborhood of New York City.

1964 **November 14** Joseph "Run" Simmons born in Queens.

1965 **January 21** Jason "Jam Master Jay" Mizell born in Brooklyn, New York.

1978 Run makes his first public performance, with Kurtis Blow.

1979 Russell Simmons releases Kurtis Blow's "Christmas Rappin."

TIMELINE

1957

October 4
Russell Simmons born in Queens, New York.

1964

May 31
Darryl "DMC" McDaniels born in the Harlem neighborhood of New York City.

November 14
Joseph "Run" Simmons born in Queens.

1957

1978

1965

January 21
Jason "Jam Master Jay" Mizell born in Brooklyn, New York.

1978
Run makes his first public performance, with Kurtis Blow.

1981   Run and DMC perform in their first public
       appearance together.

1983   Run and DMC sign with Profile Records

       April Run-DMC's first single, "It's Like That"
       is released.

1984   "Rock Box" begins heavy rotation on MTV.

       Run-DMC headlines the Fresh Fest tour.

       Run-DMC stars in *Krush Groove.*

1985   Run-DMC participates in the historic Live Aid
       benefit concert.

1983
April
Run-DMC's
first single,
"It's Like That"
is released.

1986
Run-DMC signs an endorsement
deal with Adidas.

The band collaborates with
rock group Aerosmith to make
hip-hop history.

1983   2002

1985
Run-DMC par-
ticipates in the
historic Live Aid
benefit concert.

2002
March
The band is inducted into the
Hip-Hop Hall of Fame.
October 30
Jason "Jam Master Jay" Mizell is
murdered in a Queens recording studio.

Run-DMC officially disbands.

1986 Run-DMC signs an endorsement deal with Adidas.

The band collaborates with rock group Aerosmith to make hip-hop history.

2002 **February 25** Run-DMC is the first hip-hop group to be honored on the RockWalk in Hollywood, California.

March The band is inducted into the Hip-Hop Hall of Fame.

October 30 Jason "Jam Master Jay" Mizell is murdered in a Queens recording studio.

November Jam Master Jay's funeral brings together members of the hip-hop community.

Run-DMC officially disbands.

2005 *Run's House* begins shooting.

2006 DMC meets his birth mother and founds a camp for parentless children.

GLOSSARY

backspinning Manually rotating a vinyl record in order to repeat key phrases or beats.

B-boy/B-girl Short for break boy and break girl; someone who break-dances.

blaxploitation movies A popular film genre of the 1970s targeted at urban, black audiences.

break beat The part of a dance song in which the singing stops but the percussion continues.

break dancing An acrobatic style of dancing that first developed during the mid-1970s in the predominantly African-American neighborhoods of the Bronx in New York City.

DJ Short for disc jockey; a hip-hop DJ (or spinner) creates the background music for rap songs by manipulating recordings through such techniques as audio mixing, scratching, and backspinning.

dozens Often considered a precursor of rap, the dozens is a word game dating back to the slave era in which one player taunts another by insulting or poking fun at his or her family.

emcee or MC Short for master of ceremonies, an early name for a rapper.

gangsta rap A subgenre of rap that typically includes violent and sexist lyrics.

graffiti A form of street art in which "writers" use paint or permanent markers to make distinctive designs on the sides of subway cars, buildings, and other public and private surfaces.

griot Linked by many scholars to modern rappers, the West-African griot was a traveling troubadour who both educated and entertained his listeners with stories that were usually chanted in a rhythmic fashion.

hip-hop   A cultural movement that first developed in the predominantly African-American neighborhoods of the South Bronx during the 1970s and includes four elements: graffiti, break dancing, deejaying, and rap.

rap   A genre of music in which rhymed lyrics are spoken over rhythm tracks and snippets of recorded music and sounds.

rhythm and blues (R&B)   A style of African-American music that combines elements of blues and jazz and is usually performed with electric guitars and other electrically amplified instruments.

scratching   Moving a record back and forth under a phonograph needle to create a rhythmic sound.

signifying   Often considered a precursor of rap, signifying is a traditional African-American word game in which players brags about their own assets or accomplishments while belittling those of their opponent.

toasting   A Jamaican tradition in which the DJ at a dance party talks over songs; toasting was imported to the Bronx in the early seventies where it would play a key role in the development of rap.

▸ ▸ BIBLIOGRAPHY ▪ ‖

Adler, Bill. *Tougher Than Leather: The Rise of Run DMC.* Los Angeles: Consafos Press, 1987.

Allen, Harry. "Jam Master Jay, 1965–2002." *Village Voice,* November 6–November 12, 2002, pp. 50–52.

Chang, Jeff. *Can't Stop Won't Stop: A History of the Hip-Hop Generation.* New York: St. Martin's Press, 2005.

Coleman, Mark. "Back from Hell." *Rolling Stone,* January 10, 1991, p. 66.

Fricke, Jim, and Charlie Ahearn. *Yes Yes Y'All: Oral History of Hip-Hop's First Decade.* Cambridge, MA: Da Capo Press, 2002.

Harrington, Richard. "Tougher Than Leather." *Washington Post,* September 17, 1988.

Light, Alan, ed. *The Vibe History of Hip-Hop.* New York: Three Rivers Press, 1999.

McDaniels, Darryl, with Bruce Haring. *King of Rock: Respect, Responsibility, and My Life with Run-DMC.* New York: St. Martin's Press, 2001.

Miller, Debby. "Run-DMC." *Rolling Stone,* August 30, 1984, p. 41.

Perkins, William Eric, ed. *Droppin' Science: Critical Essays on Rap Music and Hip-Hop Culture.* Philadelphia: Temple University Press, 1996.

Phinney, Kevin. *Souled America: How Black Music Transformed White Culture.* New York: Billboard Books, 2005.

Ro, Ronin. *Raising Hell: The Reign, Ruin, and Redemption of Run-D.M.C. and Jam Master Jay.* New York: Amisted, 2005.

Rose, Tricia. *Black Noise: Rap Music and Culture in Contemporary America.* Hanover, NH: Wesleyan University Press, 1994.

Simmons, Joseph "Reverend Run." *It's Like That: A Spiritual Memoir.* New York: St. Martin's, 2000.

Thigpen, David E. *Jam Master Jay: The Heart of Hip-Hop.* New York: Pocket Star Books, 2003.

Simmons, Russell, with Nelson George. *Life and Def: Sex, Drugs, Money, and God.* New York: Crown Publishers, 2001.

Green, Jared, ed. *Rap and Hip-Hop.* San Diego: Greenhaven Press, 2003.

Haskins, Jim. *One Nation Under a Groove: Rap Music and Its Roots.* New York: Hyperion, 2000.

Lommel, Cookie. *The History of Rap Music.* Philadelphia: Chelsea House, 2001.

McDaniels, Darryl, with Bruce Haring. *King of Rock: Respect, Responsibility, and My Life with Run-DMC.* New York: St. Martin's Press, 2001.

Shapiro, Peter. *The Rough Guide to Hip-Hop.* London: Rough Guides, 2005.

Simmons, Joseph "Reverend Run." *It's Like That: A Spiritual Memoir.* New York: St. Martin's, 2000.

WEB SITES

http://www.allhiphop.com
All Hiphop.com

http://www.me-dmc.com/
DMC: The Official Website of DMC (Darryl McDaniels)

http://www.rapdict.org/
The Rap Dictionary

http://www6.rsmusicgroup.com/revrun/home.php
Rev Run

http://www.rundmcmusic.com/
Run-DMC

▸ ▸ PHOTO CREDITS ■ ‖

▸ ▸ ABOUT THE AUTHORS ■ ‖

LOUISE CHIPLEY SLAVICEK received her master's degree in history from the University of Connecticut. She is the author of more than a dozen books for young people, including *Women of the American Revolution, Israel,* and *The Great Wall of China.* She lives in Ohio.

CHUCK D redefined rap music and hip-hop culture as leader and cofounder of legendary rap group Public Enemy. His messages addressed weighty issues about race, rage, and inequality with a jolting combination of intelligence and eloquence. A musician, writer, radio host, TV guest, college lecturer, and activist, he is the creator of Rapstation.com, a multiformat home on the Web for the vast global hip-hop community.